Summary

Online Forex...8

Chapter 1 - Forex: the largest financial market in the world..13

   1.1 - How to enter the Forex........................17

   1.2 - The main mechanisms that govern the Forex 21

   1.3 - The Pareto principle.............................25

   1.4 – What are currencies 30

      1.4.1 – Cross majors..................................31

      1.4.2 – Cross Minors 37

      1.4.3 – Exotic currency pairs 39

      1.4.4 – Cryptocurrencies 41

   1.5 – Observe the spread and the pip to get profits..44

   1.6 – Forex trading today 47

- Chapter 2 - How to make money in Forex 52
  - 2.1 – Implementation of a valid strategy 55
    - 2.1.1 – Money Management....................57
    - 2.1.2 – Risk Management 62
  - 2.2 – Trend analysis 68
    - 2.2.1 – Technical Analysis 70
    - 2.2.2. – Fundamental Analysis 78
  - 2.3 – The study of volatility and market expectations...84
  - 2.4 – Signal reception....................................89
- Chapter 3 – Brokers 92
  - 3.1 – Who are the brokers? 93
  - 3.2 – What role do brokers play in Forex?...94
  - 3.3 – How to invest with brokers 96
    - 3.3.1 – CFD 98
    - 3.3.2 – Binary options 99
    - 3.3.3 – Forex 100

- 3.3.4 – Social Trading 101
- 3.3 – Trading platforms...............................103
- Fundamental Analysis 105
- Chapter 1 - What is Fundamental Analysis 108
  - 1.1 – Main differences between Fundamental Analysis and Technical Analysis 116
  - 1.2 – What is the Fundamental Analysis for? 125
  - 1.3 – Data collection and analysis..............134
    - 1.3.1 – Macroeconomic data 139
    - 1.3.2 – Microeconomics data.................146
  - 1.4 – Operational difficulties in applying the Fundamental Analysis 150
- Chapter 2 - The financial statements and the Fundamental Analysis 156
  - 2.1 – Budget structure 160
    - 2.1.1 – Balance Sheet..............................162
    - 2.1.2 – Income Statement.......................165

2.1.3 – Notes to the financial statements and cash flow statement.........................169

2.2 – Analysis of the financial statement indicators useful for Fundamental Analysis 175

2.2.1 - Earning Before Interest, Taxes, Depreciation and Amortization..............176

2.2.2 – Return On Equity........................179

2.2.3 – Return On Investment................181

Chapter 3 - Fundamental Analysis in the stock market and Forex..183

3.1 – The stock market: sector analysis and company valuation 187

3.2 – The intrinsic value of equities 191

3.2.2 – The market multiples method....198

3.3 – The real estate sector 202

3.4 – Fundamental Analysis in Forex 211

3.4.1 – The Monetary Policy of the Central Banks..217

- 3.4.2 – The economy 218
- 3.4.3 – The trend in gold and oil commodities 220

Conclusions 223

Operating Forex Trading 226

Chapter 1 - What is Forex Trading 230

- 1.1 – How Forex is born 232
- 1.2 – The main advantages 241
- 1.3 – The subjects in the Forex market 247
- 1.4 – Capital management 256
- 1.5 – Forex Trading Indices 264
- 1.6 – The times at which to trade 269
  - 1.6.1 – Forex in America 271
  - 1.6.2 – Forex in Europa 273
  - 1.6.3 – Forex in Asia 275
- 2.1 – Stop-loss 279
- 2.2 – Take Profit 284

2.3 – Market orders 289

2.4 – Limit orders 292

Chapter 3 - Fundamental Analysis and Technical Analysis 296

   3.1 – Fundamental Analysis: macroeconomic indicators 302

   3.2 – The three pillars of Technical Analysis 307

   3.3 – Dow's Theory 311

   3.4 – The Momentum and Fibonacci retracements 320

   3.5 – Overbought and oversold 326

   4.1 – The moving averages 330

   4.3 – Relative Strenght Index 334

   4.4 – Adverage Directional Index 336

   4.5 – The stochastic oscillator 338

Conclusions 341

Fundamental Analysis

The origins of Fundamental Analysis date back to ancient times, but despite this, it still represents a fundamental pillar for the study and interpretation of financial assets. Being able to juggle in this type of analysis can be very useful for evaluating the economy and market sectors, to learn to manage and invest prudently and consciously their capital.

Those who intend to invest through the use of Fundamental Analysis but are not professionals in this field can find considerable difficulties. However, thanks to a study of the subject, they may be able to acquire the necessary skills to correctly interpret market signals. In fact, the assumption of this analysis is the interpretation of the data, unlike the Technical Analysis which provides the necessary indicators and resources.

The use of Fundamental Analysis can prove to be an excellent study tool, but it will be even better if it is combined with Technical Analysis in a combined way. The work of the fundamental analyst consists in fact in the research and interpretation of the financial data present in the market, of the indicators and parameters established by the Technical Analysis, to achieve the best possible results.

Chapter 1 - What is Fundamental Analysis

Every investor uses different techniques in order to try to anticipate the movements of the financial markets and thus make profits. One of the techniques most used by traders is called Fundamental Analysis. Regardless of the experience possessed by the investor, the Fundamental Analysis explains, by means of data, what is actually occurring in a given financial market, in such a way to hypothesize what could happen to the trend in subsequent periods.

Many individuals have tried several times to enter the world of trading, but having no real market analysis and money management strategy, they ended their experience with failure. In fact, observing the data provided by research institutions and bodies can prove to be a completely useless action, as the statistics are incomprehensible. An inexperienced trader will not be able to exploit this information, selecting them and inserting them in a logical scheme.

What sets Fundamental Analysis apart from any other market analysis technique is the ability to base one's strategy not on historical or past facts, but on what is happening at the exact moment you decide to invest.

Therefore, the Fundamental Analysis deals with observing and examining the business trend to study its ability to improve in the future and the ways in which it can grow. In this way, the trader has a complete picture of the market trend. Of course, it can be counterproductive to base one's strategy solely on Fundamental Analysis. It is important for a trader to amalgamate the data and statistics deriving from different analysis techniques, in such a way that will increase the chances of making successes in the performance of the trading activity.

However, it is known that many traders decide to completely omit this type of analysis, focusing on other techniques. A new trader that faces the Forex market or any other financial market also using the Fundamental Analysis can start off with other investors, managing to face other competitors and remain active on the market in the long run.

Therefore, Fundamental Analysis does not focus on the visible elements that characterize a trend, such as the price of a specific financial instrument, or on the profits that can be made from a certain investment, but rather it is based on the study of the business and on the value that the same could generate over time, if optimized correctly. This is a much broader view of the market, which makes it possible not to exclude from the analysis of some elements, sometimes fundamental, that otherwise would have been neglected.

The Fundamental Analysis is generally oriented towards the long term, as it is impossible to identify what the trend of the trend may be in the short term, since the business is a very variable datum and prone to seasonal changes, mainly due to the strategies adopted by the companies.

Ultimately, the Fundamental Analysis deals with analyzing and studying what the health status of a given company or a financial asset is. The Fundamental Analysis must be applied in a constant manner, in such a way to verify whether the well-being of the company or if the market is growing or falling and what are the consequences of some economic events on it. The trader must be aware of all the elements that characterize the assets and the economy of the company, but also the performance of the latter, which can only be examined by applying a series of indices to the items that make up the financial statements.

- The Fundamental Analysis aims, according to the company or asset analyzed, a series of objectives, which can help the trader to make the correct investment decisions:
- - First of all, the evaluation of the business, in order to guarantee greater probabilities of profit in the performance of long-term trading;
- - Secondly, the assessment of the macroeconomic trend, with in-depth analysis of the aspects relating to local production, which are able to influence

the performance of the company or asset;
- - Thirdly, the assessment of the administrative and strategic choices of each company capable of influencing the asset, but also of the decisions taken by political leaders with the focus of the effects of these choices on the market;
- - Finally, the detailed evaluation of the relationship between yield and risk, with the study of all the elements that can alter this relationship and with the analysis of future events that could affect it.

1.1 – Main differences between Fundamental Analysis and Technical Analysis

The Fundamental Analysis, for the characteristics and objects taken into consideration, represents the antithesis of Technical Analysis. The latter is used by traders to investigate the historical price trend of a given financial instrument, so as to identify a match in the behavior of the trend, and on the basis of this, hypothesize what its future evolution will be. Therefore, the Technical Analysis does not turn its gaze towards the business and the financial statement ratios but focuses its attention on the prices and the charts that show the fluctuations of the same.

The entire Technical Analysis is based on the concept that all men, and in particular those who act within financial markets, perform their actions repetitively. This idea is linked in particular to the fact that human actions are driven by instinct. When the trend is favorable, uncontrollable euphoria leads subjects to open more and more positions; conversely, the depression due to the inability to anticipate the evolution of the trend leads traders to close positions. These two emotions, completely irrational, are implemented in an almost monotonous manner, pushing the trend up or down. The Technical Analysis tries to understand what the mood of the traders is, so as to anticipate the evolution of the trend.

All this is not contemplated by the Fundamental Analysis, which focuses solely on the data released and made public by the statistical authorities and the financial statements of the individual financial companies. This information, however, is considered incomplete and will have to be analyzed with the help of formulas relating to financial mathematics.

A further distinction between these two types of analysis is represented by the moment in which the entry or exit from the market is decided. In fact, the technical analyst awaits the opening, or closing, of a position until the price has assumed a certain value. This implies that the trader must constantly and almost obsessively observe the trend of the trend and the evolution of the price level. An alternative method is to rely on Trading System, that is automated systems that act completely independently on the financial market on the basis of the strategy set by the investor. The Fundamental Analysis refers to two elements present in the market: the actual value of the asset and the market value. When the actual value is higher than the market value, the fundamental analyst tends to open a position in the market. Vice versa, the position must be closed when the market value exceeds the actual value.

Going deeper into these two different approaches to the market, it is possible to state that the fundamental analyst concentrates his or her forces in the initial phase of trading, namely that of collecting data and studying information, while a greater effort is required from the technical analyst. Moment of observation of the trend, that is during the phase immediately preceding that of entry or exit from the market. In the latter case, however, stress could easily lead the trader to error: the markets are excessively agitated and seizing the right moment to make his choice can be really complicated.

In general, however, it is impossible to define a priori which is the best analysis technique between the two, as both types are linked to external factors and to the risk appetite possessed by the individual investor. An excellent trader is aware of the fact that both Fundamental and Technical Analyses are very important to achieve success in the world of trading and for this reason, the best choice is to use both techniques depending on the situation, or even combine them to increase your chances of making a profit.

Naturally, regardless of the analysis for which one opts, it is fundamental to support each of them with a correct strategy of capital management and risk management. Furthermore, the trader must always take into account the volatility present in the markets, and on the basis of each element make his own choice of investment.

As said, the Technical Analysis and the Fundamental Analysis can be thought of as two opposite categories of market interpretation, but not for this reason, the trader must not use them in a combined manner. In fact, carrying out both types of analysis can bring advantages, as the investor can get a clear idea of the market, both in the short and medium-term, and in the long term.

One of the strategies most used by traders in both Forex and other financial markets is to allocate a certain amount of money on the market and use it following the guidelines indicated in the Technical

Analysis, while the remaining part must be invested according to the concepts inherent in Fundamental Analysis. It is an indirect attempt to reach profitability in the short-term, following the Technical Analysis, and in the long-term, following the Fundamental Analysis.

1.2 – What is the Fundamental Analysis for?

Fundamental Analysis can also be used in areas other than trading. Many managers, for example, use the concepts belonging to this approach to obtain predictions that are probable but not certain on certain economic activities that are somehow related to their company. By broadening the vision of the economic world, it is possible to apply Fundamental Analysis for everyday choices, sometimes even trivial ones, which represent the lives of individuals. In this way, the vision of the future may appear less uncertain and certainly brighter.

Fundamental analysis can also be exploited by individual workers. An employee of a company can analyze the financial statements and all the financial information that must be made public in a mandatory way in order to guess the future of the company in which he or she works and, consequently, his or her future.

Generally, professionals and entrepreneurs can also obtain advantages, anticipating any crisis in the sector. The ability to obtain and understand certain information can allow these subjects to search for differentiation in the market, in such a way to grab as many customers as possible and face the possible crisis in the best way.

Fundamental Analysis can also be used to study the future benefits related to the purchase of a durable good. Whether it is a company or any private entity, the purchase of an asset of this kind must be sufficiently weighted. But an analysis of this kind can also be carried out by a selling company, which studies the financial and economic possibilities of potential customers. Not only that, many physical and juridical subjects analyze the state of health of financial institutions to understand which is the best institution in which to deposit their savings.

To be able to realize all this, however, the Fundamental Analysis must be structured on the basis of some passages, which if carried out correctly, guarantee their full effectiveness.

One of the first steps that every trader or any other person must implement involves the collection of data to be subjected to analysis, relating to a given asset, to a company or a financial institution. Thanks to the advent of the internet, today's subjects are able to find the data necessary to carry out a study of this kind very easily, in particular by browsing the web pages of the various national and international government institutions.

A second step can be identified in the surveys carried out by the interested parties directly in the places of activity. This means that if a trader decides to analyze a particular business in such a way to evaluate the entry into the market, he or she must go to the financial and legal offices of the various companies that characterize this business and verify what the actual influx of customers is, or the breadth of availability of products to sell or even the methods of corporate organization adopted by individual companies.

Once the statistical and visual data are obtained, the fundamental analyst must organize them, subdividing them according to financial nature. Generally, the data are assigned to two categories: the macroeconomic one and the microeconomic one. However, each subject may decide to make a different subdivision according to their needs. To carry out this step, it is necessary to rely on electronic worksheets.

However, the fundamental analyst must continue his or her work of data collection. In fact, it is important to read up on all the competing companies present on the assets to verify what their real state of health is, but above all their attitude. There are indeed market phases during which the companies appear to be aggressive, and deciding to open certain financial positions during these periods can prove counterproductive. The data collected must be used to make comparisons, known to experts as benchmark.

In reality, the data collection phase can be considered infinite for those who decide to rely on Fundamental Analysis. Naturally, once the past and present data of the companies, competitors and financial institutions have been collected, it will only be a work of updating, which involves less effort than that carried out in the initial phase of the study.

Some fundamental analysts, especially if they are inexperienced, decide to skip or otherwise underestimate these steps. In reality, without a statistical basis and a clear view of the market situation and the state of health of competing companies, it is impossible to relate the asset to its market value, to understand if one is in a moment of underestimation or overestimation of the same.

An approach of this kind leads the fundamental analyst to have advantages over any other subject. However, this advantage must be maintained over time, through correct capital management, effective risk management and constant updating of data.

1.3 – Data collection and analysis

As mentioned above, the internet and the various websites represent the main source from which to draw the statistical, patrimonial and economic data useful for achieving a correct Fundamental Analysis. Therefore, it is advisable to mark each individual web page in an economic calendar, in which all the dates of publication of the information necessary for analysis are reported.

In particular, the fundamental analyst must search for all the monetary policy announcements, relating to data or information, which are periodically released by the individual national central banks. Furthermore, the quarterly data relating to the GDP trend, that is the Gross Domestic Product, of each nation, which indicates the health status and the economic evolution, are fundamental. Finally, depending on the type of Fundamental Analysis carried out, it is necessary to collect data relating to the production of the manufacturing sector only and, consequently, of all the production that does not derive from this sector, in particular, that relating to the industrial sector and the service sector or services. But not only. It is important not to underestimate the data relating to inflation in a given State, an element that greatly conditions the price trend on the various assets, but also those that refer to the employment and welfare of a country. Finally, the fundamental analyst must collect the data that allow to obtain the indices representative of the trust of companies and consumers, the data reported on the balance sheets of companies or other economic and patrimonial data that are released by the institutions or by the companies in a periodic manner, such as the data relating to forecasts on future market trends that are issued by the European Commission.

It is also advisable to find pure statistics and data, which have not already been analyzed and interpreted by the press, as the business or asset situation may have been altered, even unintentionally. Other times the difficulty of finding information is linked to the difference in language, especially if it involves investments to be made in Asian countries. So if you are not able to interpret a language, an investment of this kind could turn out to be really very dangerous, not having a Fundamental Analysis of support and a well-studied strategy behind it.

The creation of an economic calendar, therefore, represents one of the first necessary steps in order to organize one's data collection activity. You can download already compiled calendars online, but they will have to be updated and increased based on your needs.

Once a calendar of this kind has been created, it is possible to analyze the various macroeconomic and microeconomic data present in each individual asset.

1.3.1 – Macroeconomic data

Macroeconomics is considered a branch of financial matter that deals with the analysis of some basic measures to carry out a correct fundamental analysis.

First of all, macroeconomics is concerned with assessing the relationship between national debt and Gross Domestic Product, to understand the actual evolutionary trend of a State.

Secondly, macroeconomics considers what the national employment rate is. This rate can be broken down by age and by seasonal period in order to carry out different investigations. The rate of inflation is also one of the basic indicators of Fundamental Analysis. This rate must be relatively low to prevent the currency from losing value, but not too low as a State with an inflation rate that tends to zero risks ending up in a recession. Finally, macroeconomics deals with the rate of economic growth, which shows the extent to which a country can obtain benefits in the future and achieve certain objectives.

Each of these rates or ratios allows the fundamental analyst to assess the course of a given economic reality. However, macroeconomics does not refer to individual activities, but to markets considered as aggregate systems. Therefore, the analyst is required to combine the individual company outputs in order to guess what the economic evolution in a given asset may be. The analysis must be carried out considering the pure data, not processed by other bodies or agencies.

There are numerous reports, also available online, which offer some interpretations of asset trends. However, these interpretations may prove to be inaccurate, and for this reason, it is important to rely on one's own skills rather than on those made available by external parties. Furthermore, these reports can refer to time horizons different from those set by the analyst. In this sense, the interpretations will be different, being based on completely different logics.

In this logic, it becomes important to divide the trade into two components: the liquid capital, represented by payments and receipts, and the deferred capital, represented by investments, credits, and debts. In addition to this, the analyst must also evaluate the national balance of payments, to see if the value of exports exceeds that of imports.

However, fundamental analysts can use systems that simplify data and economic reality. In particular, there are two models that perform this task effectively, namely Investment Saving - Liquidity Money, known with the acronym IS-LM, and the Aggregate Supply - Aggregate Demand, known more simply as AD-AS. The first of these two models has the task of identifying which is the balance point on an economic level, considering this level to determine the starting pointto make forecasts in the medium term. The second model, on the other hand, focuses attention on the individual processes that bring the market to a certain equilibrium point and tries to understand why these processes occur. However, it is wrong to exclude completely from the analysis obtained with these models the fluctuations that characterize the market in the short term. In fact, these are very important to be able to define the trend in the market in wider horizons.

Therefore, the analysis of macroeconomic data is fundamental to understand what is the evolution of some assets or of an entire financial market, but also of much wider economic realities. An analysis based on this information can lead to surprising results, which can confirm or contradict the results of microeconomic analysis, but which nonetheless offers very important interpretations to understand what the market trend may be in the long term. It also considers some unexpected events.

The advantage of Fundamental Analysis of macroeconomic data is represented by the possibility of easily and at any time receiving information and data relating to the economic realities observed.

1.3.2 – Microeconomics data

Microeconomics stands in contrast to macroeconomics, as it analyzes individual economic realities, evaluating their evolution over time. In particular, microeconomics studies and focuses on trends in the market of single individuals, understood as consumers of goods produced by companies and services offered by them, but also of individual companies, in the dual role of suppliers and customers, and finally organizations and public and private institutions.

It is important for the fundamental analyst to understand that macroeconomic data do not have a real meaning unless they are accompanied by microeconomic ones. If a single company, even if rather large, dismisses some of its employees, this choice will have no repercussions on macroeconomic data. At the same time, however, if the layoffs concern several companies, then the employment rate, understood as a macroeconomic quantity will be influenced by varying its value.

In any case, it is always good to compare and integrate the data held, in such a way to understand in greater detail what the current market trend is.

The fundamental analysts study the microeconomic data knowing a concept that is at the base of this environment, that is what the subjects carry out every single action searching for profit. So every company sells a certain product within the market at a price that is certainly higher than the sum of the individual costs incurred to produce it. If this does not happen, the company will face a loss, and in the microeconomic world, this cannot be accepted. Loss-making companies are destined to leave the market. Once they reach a certain threshold, they are no longer able to sustain the expenses. Therefore, investors will be required to select only those investments that guarantee a sufficient probability of gain in the long term, while they will have to resist the temptation to make some investments just following their own instincts.

This temptation, which often results in bankruptcy investments, arise in delicate moments crossed by traders. They have chosen the wrong business to entrust their money to and try to remedy the initial mistake by increasing the risk of their investment.

1.4 – Operational difficulties in applying the Fundamental Analysis

The difficulties deriving from the application of the Fundamental Analysis mean that there are many who despise it in favor of Technical Analysis. But in reality, this complexity is the reason most of these people are unable to use this type of analysis. In fact, if in the Technical Analysis, it is sufficient to study the various indicators and become familiar with them, in the Fundamental Analysis, it is essential to interpret the signals on the basis of the economic, financial and social variables that can intervene in a given context or market. This interpretation is operationally very complex as it goes beyond logic, and it is not easy to manage not to be conditioned by emotions in favor of rationality. A rumor is enough to influence the market and prices.

Therefre, the interpretation represents the main operational difficulty of the Fundamental Analysis, and becomes even more complex due to the high number of data to be analyzed, quantifiable in thousands of thousands of indicators, which could influence and positively or negatively affect prices. To overcome this problem, fundamental analysts try to circumscribe the most important data to facilitate at least part of the entire analysis procedure.

The Fundamental Analysis deals with the study of the macroeconomic and microeconomic reference environment based on a well-defined econometric model that identifies the relationships between the analyzed economic realities. However, these models are not flexible, or rather only if they are applied in decisions regarding the choices of national economic policy made by governments. If they are used to operate in the financial markets, such models are not easily adaptable as they are composed of variables that cannot be controlled over time and because of their specificity towards one market rather than another. Furthermore, due to the amount of data to be adapted, the signals will not be timely.

For this reason, it is necessary to havean in-depth knowledge of mathematics, the market, econometrics, and a marked predisposition for the interpretation of data.

Sector and company analyze also present difficulties in identifying the possible financial, economic and equity scenarios of companies to estimate the income flows related to equities in the most correct way. To do this, those who decide to invest in the market using Fundamental Analysis can use supports, free or paid, that provide information, but which are however far from what is offered by the various brokers.

Various websites have been created around the world that provide a useful database for those who want to make online trading operations in an informed way, such as Financialweb, but in Europe, there are still no such sites.

The knowledge of financial analysis is a prerequisite for Fundamental Analysis, made starting from the company balance sheets and the market, through the various indices of appreciation, but the brokers rarely offer tools of this type. Therefore, the only way to correctly implement the Fundamental Analysis is to become good fundamental analysts.

Chapter 2 - The financial statements and the Fundamental Analysis

The Fundamental Analysis is based on one of the main tools used in the entire economic environment, that is the financial statements. The main purpose of this document is to show all stakeholders, internal and external, the economic and financial performance of the company. It reacts to a sort of guarantee that the company shows to every potential customer or investor. Furthermore, this document allows the company that prepares it to manage its business properly. However, it is a legal obligation for listed companies to prepare and publish the financial statements, which must be made available to each individual investor or interested party. Furthermore, the opening of companies to international markets has obliged the law to attempt to standardize these information documents to facilitate a comparison between the financial statements of different companies or between the financial statements of the same company in different periods. Of course, a comparison of this kind can only be made between companies in the same sector.

In reality, many fundamental analysts fail to carry out an analysis based on the balance sheet, as they often do not have the necessary skills to read the indices in the most appropriate way, misinterpreting the company's performance. At other times, the balance sheet can be drafted in a rather confusing manner, which removes potential investors.

In order to understand more quickly the state of health of a given economic reality, it is useful to focus on three documents of the financial statements, namely the Balance Sheet, the Income Statement and the financial statement ratios.

2.1 – Budget structure

The Balance Sheet and the Income Statement are the main documents of the financial statements and are accompanied, in order to be explained and integrated by the Explanatory Note and the Cash Flow Statement.

The Balance Sheet presents a structure with opposite sections. In the first part, that is to the left of the prospectus, are the activities; on the right, there are the liabilities. The total of the two sections must correspond to have a correct Balance Sheet.

The income statement, on the other hand, has a scalar form, divided into four sections. As we proceed in the preparation of the Income Statement, various fundamental elements are highlighted to be able to proceed with analyzing the financial statements using the indicators.

Both the Balance Sheet and the Income Statement must then be reclassified, so as to highlight further elements, which in the previous draft could not be shown.

2.1.1 – Balance Sheet

The Balance Sheet deals with grouping all the active and passive elements of a company. The active elements include investments, fixed assets, whether they be tangible, intangible or financial, current assets, consisting of inventories, receivables, and cash. Among the passive elements, on the other hand, are the shareholders' equity, the provisions for risks and charges, the severance pay and the debts. In addition to these elements, accruals and deferrals must also be appropriately divided between assets and liabilities depending on the financial event.

The net assets will be the result of the difference between active and passive elements. In this way, the interested party will be able to understand what the actual business value is once all the debts recorded in the financial statements have been settled. Therefore, the net assets show how much equity the company owns for the realization of a production phase, and by exclusion, how much are the external sources of financing owned by the company. Naturally, a healthy company must act relying only on the capital already in its possession, without relying on loans or financing received from credit institutions.

Therefore, the final objective of the Balance Sheet of the financial statements is to highlight both the capital structure and the financial situation of a particular company. It is for this reason that the balance sheet is considered as one of the main documents that must necessarily be examined by fundamental analysts.

2.1.2 – Income Statement

The Income Statement is composed of all the items relating to costs and revenues that have occurred in a specific period of time, which generally coincides with a calendar year. By observing the Profit and Loss Account, it is possible to guess whether the company has made a profit during the financial year, that is if it is a profitable company, or if it has incurred losses. In rare cases, the company closes the budget with a draw, that is with perfect equality between costs and revenues.

Defining how much profit or loss a company has is very simple. It is necessary to add revenues and costs algebraically. If a positive value is obtained, that is if the revenues exceed the costs, then there is a profit; vice versa, if the revenues are lower than the costs, there will be loss.

However, the Income Statement provides many other interesting data for the potential investor. First of all, it is possible to break down the economic results according to the product or the company production sector. In this way, it is possible to guess which product is considered the company's flagship, the new products launched on the market and even the weak points of the company. Furthermore, through the Income Statement, it is possible to analyze the company assets, comparing them with the profits made.

Another aspect linked to the Income Statement is the ability to demonstrate to all interested parties the quality of the work performed by each individual manager, depending on the functions performed. The management aspects of an enterprise are one of the most important and at the same time the most underestimated aspects within an asset. In reality, the actual performance of a company depends on the ideas and strategies implemented by these subjects. These strategies will have to deal with customers, suppliers and above all, competitors, and lead the company to optimize profit. But the goal is not always achieved.

The main difference between the Balance Sheet and the Income Statement is that the former offers a static view of a company's assets, that is, asseststhat are held at the time the financial statements are drawn up and therefore at the end of the year, while the latter analyzes and represents an economic situation evolving during the year, that is, the income stream.

2.1.3 – Notes to the financial statements and cash flow statement

Although less important for the achievement of the objectives set by a fundamental analyst, the financial statements also comprise two other documents, namely the Notes to the Financial Statements and the Financial Statement.

The Notes to the Financial Statements show all the parties involved how to implement the financial statements and what the principles adopted in it are. It also has the function of explaining individual items in a timely and detailed manner. Therefore, this document plays a fundamental role in the standardization of financial statements. In fact, the principles on which a budget is drawn up are different and follow completely different approaches and logic, depending on their vision of the market and the economy. Therefore, it is opportune to specify which of these ways the managers have adopted for the realization of the budget and how each item must be interpreted by the interested subjects.

The Financial Statement, on the other hand, is a document that in Italy has become mandatory only in the year 2015, but which nevertheless plays an important role in the interpretation of the financial statements. Its objective is to describe the liquid assets, breaking them down and analyzing them, in such a way to offer a clear and lucid vision both on the amount and on their evolution, as the values present at the beginning and end of the year are indicated. In addition, the Financial Statement analyzes the financial flows deriving from the individual company sectors, specifically from that relating to the operating activity, from the investment sectors, and from the financing sectors. The importance of this document is to guarantee the fundamental analyst a dynamic view of corporate income. Indeed, the stock of assets, static, does not allow us to investigate the trend and performance of the company in the market, and therefore offers only a limited analysis of the state of health of the company. Therefore, it is necessary to deepen the flows and analyze them in detail, in order to guess what the real business trend may be.

Furthermore, the preparation of the financial statements is based on the application of certain principles established by national law or by international regulation. The most important are those relating to prudence, which implies that only certain positive components must be reported in the financial statements, while negative ones can also be presumed; to the economic competence, which implies that only the charges and revenues pertaining to the financial year must be entered, regardless of the moment in which they will have financial manifestation; the prevalence of the substance over the form, based on which it is necessary to take into account the economic function of the individual items.

2.2 – Analysis of the financial statement indicators useful for Fundamental Analysis

The budget analysis is a very complex step, which requires technical skills and in-depth knowledge of the subject. The purpose is to obtain information that otherwise cannot be known: in particular, it involvess data concerning the management of the company. The analysis focuses on the items present in the Balance Sheet and the Income Statement relating to the year in closing and offers important indications, very useful to the fundamental analyst, which reveal the true state of health of the company. To be able to use them, however, it is necessary to re-elaborate and reclassify the financial statements according to various methods, depending on the aim pursued and the elements that we intend to investigate.

2.2.1 - Earning Before Interest, Taxes, Depreciation and Amortization

The first important financial statement indicator is called the Earning Before Interest, Taxes, Depreciation and Amortization, better known with the acronym EBITDA. The aim is to offer the fundamental analyst an objective view of the amount of wealth that has been produced by the company, only in its characteristic sector, namely the main one. It is also known as Gross Operating Margin, or simply as MOL. In reality, this indicator exploits the reclassification of the Income Statement according to the Added Value criterion to obtain an intermediate result, the result of which is solely the operational management, without the interest expense, taxes, depreciation and amortization being still covered.

An advantage offered by the calculation of the EBITDA is represented by the possibility of easily comparing the Gross Operating Margin of a financial statement with that present in the other financial statements, so as to immediately have a clear vision of the company that shows the best operating performance. In fact, the standardization of EBITDA has been carried out over the years precisely to favor a comparison by investors, but also by fundamental analysts, who base their profits on the study of company characteristics.

2.2.2 – Return On Equity

The Return On Equity indicator, better known as ROE, is one of the return on equity ratios. This indicator is used to analyze the profitability of a company in percentage terms, as it compares Net Income to Net Capital. Therefore, it indicates how much percentage of investment has translated into income. To get real information on the performance of the company, however, it is necessary to compare the value of the ROE obtained with the various investment indicators to be able to identify the opportunity cost linked to the initial investment of the company. The difference arising from this comparison is defined in the economic sphere as a risk premium. If this assumes a value of zero, then it means that it would be useless to invest in that company, as the investor would obtain the same result by not making any investment.

2.2.3 – Return On Investment

The Return On Investment indicator, also known as the ROI acronym, aims to highlight the economic efficiency of a particular company, taking into consideration only the management characteristic. The ROI does not consider the sources that are used to reach the income produced during the year. Consequently, this indicator is used by fundamental analysts to understand what the return on invested capital is.

To achieve its objective, the ROI compares the total operating result obtained by the company with the average of the capital invested during the same period.

However, the fundamental analyst must take into account certain defects in this indicator. First of all, the ROI increases with the passing of the financial years, as the balance sheet will always suffer more from the increase in the value of depreciation. A second negative point concerning ROI is that it relates a stock value, that is, the invested capital, to a flow, that is, the operating income produced.

Chapter 3 - Fundamental Analysis in the stock market and Forex

The Fundamental Analysis and the Technical Analysis represent the best methodologies to analyze the evolution of the financial markets and, in particular, of the Forex market. Without these two approaches, traders would not have a solid basis on which to make their predictions, and investments could prove bankrupt. Traders rely in particular on Fundamental Analysis to try to predict what the trend of a given trend may be in the long run.

Naturally, the Fundamental Analysis carried out on the financial markets will focus attention on the price levels of financial instruments, securities and currencies present in the market on which the trader intends to invest. It is natural, however, that an analysis of this kind can only be carried out by an experienced trader or by real analysts who carry out these studies by profession. This is because inexperienced investors do not have sufficient skills to correctly describe the economic events that can affect the financial market.

Generally, the Fundamental Analysis applied on the financial markets focuses on the macroeconomic causes, that is, on all those events able to modify the curve of the demand and that of the offer even in the largest financial market in the world, namely the Forex. Thus the fundamental analyst turns his or her gaze towards the progress of the individual nations, but also towards a homogeneous trend that can bring together a group of states that have similar geographical, ethnic or cultural features, or towards the entire world economic evolution. However, what mostly influences the financial market are the decisions taken by national and international political leaders. In fact, they have direct influences on the economic results of the individual states, since the correlation between the world of politics and that of finance is direct. Further aspects that affect the fundamental analysis are the impacts of the social world and even of the climate, both on trade and on the price of goods. These are aspects that should not be underestimated, which can often help the trader to understand in advance the future market swings, thus generating more profits.

3.1 – The stock market: sector analysis and company valuation

One of the objectives of a fundamental analyst is to understand what the real value of the shares is, in order to compare it with the value expressed on the market. In this way, the trader has the opportunity to invest in undervalued securities, assuming that they will soon take their real value, thanks to the classic financial corrections of the market. The Fundamental Analysis approach to the stock market is based on a series of steps that every investor must put into practice.

The first phase refers to the analysis of all the macroeconomic scenarios that can influence the stock market. First of all, this analysis must be subdivided by geographical area and by economic area. In this way, the trader can opt for the markets considered more favorable, depending on the results of the analysis.

The second phase involves sectoral analysis. This is a complex study, as it considers all the businesses present on the market in which it has chosen to invest and examines all possible future scenarios. The sectoral analysis goes beyond the world strictly linked to the economy and finance, as it encompasses social, IT, political and cultural subjects. Of course, to carry out an analysis of this kind, one requires certain skills and a thorough knowledge of the stock market.

The third and final phase involves the evaluation of the companies present on the market. This means that the trader must evaluate the financial statements made public by each company, must reclassify the Balance Sheet and the Income Statement and on these statements must apply the financial statement ratios. In this way, the investor will be able to understand what the real value of the company is. This value must then be compared to the quotation that the company expresses on the market, and on the difference arising from it, the trader will be able to make an investment with a much higher probability of a positive outcome.

3.2 – The intrinsic value of equities

One of the most important steps in the whole Fundamental Analysis is for a trader to understand what it means to analyze the intrinsic value of a given asset. The definition of intrinsic value takes on a rather simple meaning to understand from a theoretical point of view, but in practice, it can be very difficult to obtain.

However, it is necessary to start from the assumption that the intrinsic value of a given financial instrument or of a certain asset is a conceptually utopian value. In fact, this value would be possible in reality only if all investors were totally rational subjects, who do not make mistakes and who efficiently act on perfect benchmarks. Only in this way, in fact, could the actual value of a financial product or a market be obtained.

Identifying this value is however possible, at least hypothetically, and it is above all extremely advantageous. To do this, a fundamental analyst should sift through a business in every area, from the management to the strategies adopted, from the investments made to the financial statements, taking into account the sources from which the financial resources are drawn and their ability to turn into income. Once the analyst has an idea of what the intrinsic price of a certain economic reality may be, he or she will have to analyze the value it has assumed on the market and based on this, he or she will have to make his or her own investment. The basic concept on which to base his or her trading, however, is that in the long term the price taken by a financial asset and its intrinsic value will tend to coincide. So if the value assumed in the market by the business is lower than the calculated intrinsic value, then the analyst will be oriented to buying the stock, knowing that probably in the long run these will correspond.

Therefore, it is possible to affirm that the determination of the intrinsic value of a stock or asset can represent the main objective of the entire Fundamental Analysis. Once the investor has become aware of this data, in fact, he or she may decide to make his or her own investment or not, knowing already, if it has been correctly counted, what the probable future trend of the price observed in the market will be.

It is for this reason that the experts in the field have tried to create different models that help the investor to trace more quickly to the intrinsic value. Some models, however, involve rather complex passages, which can lead to error and to obtain a completely inaccurate result.

However, it is possible to bring the models back to only two types: the Dividend Discount Models, also known as dividend discounting models, and the Stock Market Multiples, known as models of market multiples. Each of these models has undergone important changes over the years, which have led to an overall optimization of the entire Fundamental Analysis.

3.2.1 - The dividend discounting model

The Dividend Discount Models focus on the discounting of the final price of a specific financial instrument and on the discounting of all dividends that have been paid in a given time interval, which coincides with the period of ownership of the same instrument. This discounting inevitably depends on an interest rate, which must be calculated by relying on additional analysis tools, such as the CAPM model (Capital Asset Pricing Model).

The logic that characterizes this model is based on the knowledge and the study of balance sheet data made public by the companies, from which it is possible to infer a hypothetical intrinsic value of financial security. The value obtained is to be compared with that on the market, both to understand if it is actually reliable, and to guess whether the business is undervalued or overvalued.

3.2.2 – The market multiples method

The same results obtained with the dividend discounting method can also be reached with the market multiples method, which is one of the most used methods by traders to make a correct business valuation. This system bases its approach on the valuation of the prices of goods produced by similar companies belonging to the same sector. The prices analyzed are related to the items in the financial statements, in particular, the profit, but also to the EBITDA, EBIT and shareholders' equity. From this relationship, different multiples arise.

The most important and most used multiple by traders is relative to the ratio between price and the average profit of the sector. Generally, the historical profit is used, but the best indication is obtained by comparing the price to the expected profit for the current year. This market multiple provides important information regarding the number of years necessary to repay with just the profits the investments made by the company. A low value of the report indicates that the company is undervalued, conversely high values indicate that there is an overvaluation. However, there is no standard value that the trader can consider as an optimal point, but the evaluation of the multiple must be compared with the reference sector. In fact, a mature sector has lower price-earnings ratios while, due to the great expectations of growth, the young sectors have a much higher average ratio.

Also multiple refers to the relationship between price and equity. It is possible to obtain the net assets both from the difference between assets and liabilities and by adding the reserves indicated in the statement to the share capital. This business valuation method is generally used to analyze the real value held by financial, insurance or banking companies. This report helps the trader to understand the price at which the market is willing to pay a surplus with respect to the value of the company assets.

If the report gives a result lower than 1, then the company is undervalued and therefore a lower value is expressed on the market than the real one. If, on the other hand, the value generates a value of less than 0.5, the company's valuation is very bad and the multiple even indicates a high risk of a real crisis.

3.3 – The real estate sector

One of the main indicators of the state of health of a market is certainly the real estate sector. This represents one of the most abundant sources from which a trader can draw a lot of information, especially in relation to long-term investments.

The importance of the real estate sector is derived mainly from the massive influence it expresses both at the macroeconomic level and at the microeconomic level. In particular, the first is one of the main indicators of the development perspectives that an economy can conceal, while the second is an indicator of the portfolio values present among private individuals.

Generally, the real estate sector considers real estate as an evaluation unit, made up of both land and a building erected on it. However, the assessment ignores this consideration and focuses attention on the intended use, that is, it evaluates whether the property is for commercial use or simply residential.

As with almost any other asset, even in the real estate sector, it is possible to make long-term investments, or speculative investments to be converted into profits in the short and medium term. In particular, an investor speculates in the real estate sector by buying a property at a lower price than its real value, which can happen for example during a real estate auction, and then resell the same property at the right price, in the shortest possible time.

What further links the real estate sector with the financial market is the provision of credits. In fact, the purchase, construction or renovation of a property are the main reasons why a funding body grants a loan to a private individual, while the purchase or realization of productive properties is the basic reason for the granting of corporate mortgages or for the stipulation of leasing contracts. It is because of the close link between real estate and interest expense, property prices are subject to strong volatility, a characteristic that can have significant influences on the stock market. In fact, banks and credit institutions have a variable reserve, linked to the quality of the credits that are provided. Any devaluations on the real estate market can generate very negative consequences, which can lead to even very serious financial crises, such as that occurred in the United States in 2009.

Therefore, a fundamental analyst must constantly monitor the entire real estate sector in order to understand which events can affect the financial markets and which ones can have only relative effects. To facilitate this task, each state has created a system that constantly monitors the real estate sector. These systems allow you to acquire certain periodic information, monthly or quarterly depending on the country, on the various municipalities, cities, urban conglomerates, and metropolitan cities. With this data, the analyst can more easily and more precisely guess what the current price trend is within the market and can create forecasts about its possible future developments.

The organization that plays this role in the United States is the S&P Case, while in the European territory, the Eurostat provides the necessary data. In Japan, the studymade available to all potential analysts, traders and investors is carried out directly by the Ministry that deals with both the territorial situation and the infrastructures. The latter has divided the analysis of the real estate market into two different categories: the first is dedicated exclusively to in-depth analyses carried out on the market, but also to the interpretations relating to the trends of the various trends, while the second is dedicated to pure statistical data.

To open an investment of real estate type, it is possible to adopt two different types of execution. The first is direct and requires a rather large capital reserve and constant and active management of the investment. The allocated capital can be either own or derived from loans or loans granted. The second method involves the possibility of buying the property without holding the pure property, but only a portion of a fund. For many reasons, the use of mutual funds differs from the first. In fact, this second way of opening an investment requires much less time and much less dedication. Furthermore, the costs related to the management and to the various commissions related to the project will be divided according to the quota held. Another advantage is a possibility of dividing the risk. In fact, a real estate fund of this kind involves the subdivision of capital over a very large number of assets, thus also favoring the possibility of investing in foreign markets that are also very distant.

In addition to direct information, the real estate sector also offers some indirect information, which must be received and examined by the fundamental analyst. In fact, the real estate indexes can be used as real benchmarks, constituting a very interesting basis of analysis to guess what the future trends of the various financial instruments observed may be.

3.4 – Fundamental Analysis in Forex

Even in Forex, fundamental analysts have the objective of understanding what the future trend in the prices of financial instruments in the market may be. In order to achieve this goal, however, it is necessary to take into account different aspects, which constantly affect the market and which sanction the path followed by financial trends.

One of the first aspects that every fundamental analyst must necessarily study is the interest rate. The value of this element is decided by the central banks of each nation, which acts according to the logic adopted by the various governments. Therefore, it is inevitable that the choices made in this area have some influence on the Forex market, especially if it is a state that has some influence at the world level.

Inflation is another element that should not be underestimated. This quantifies the value and the purchasing power of money and is, therefore, a fundamental aspect of every financial market. Also, in this case, the governments, through different maneuvers, influence the rate of inflation, knowing that a high rate leads to a halt in consumption, while an excessively low rate leads to recession.

Naturally, every fundamental analyst who acts in the Forex market must necessarily relate to the national Gross Domestic Product. Analyzing this element is indispensable in order to understand what the level of volatility on the market is. Moreover, GDP is considered one of the most important indicators of the economic performance of a nation. Fundamental analysts can also use preliminary GDP ratios, without waiting for the official report, in order to anticipate a possible trend reversal, obtaining substantial profits.

But Forex also has its roots in society, and for this reason, the unemployment rate is one of the most influential indicators of financial instrument price trends. In addition to representing another important indicator of the health status of a nation, the unemployment rate also outlines the average wealth held by individual citizens, which affect national consumption and GDP.

A nation with excellent social and economic welfare also shows a positive trade balance, obtained from the difference between imports and exports made in a given period. Moreover, if imports exceed exports, the value of the currency is strengthened, while in the opposite case the currency will be weakened.

Even the stability of governments is one of the main elements that determine the fluctuations within Forex. Naturally, the trust placed by individual traders in domestic financial stocks causes prices to fluctuate.

In addition to all these indicators and situations, each trader will have to focus his or her financial analysis on three other elements. These in fact, directly and indirectly, influence the market and require a detailed and non-negligible examination.

3.4.1 – The Monetary Policy of the Central Banks

The analysis of the Monetary Policy moves implemented by the individual central banks is fundamental to understand the real possibilities that within a state a tendency towards economic growth can be generated. The Monetary Policy does not only act in the sphere of inflation and interest rates but also deals with the relationship with other states, technology, investments, and even social welfare. Therefore, it is a very broad discipline that embraces almost every aspect of the economy. However, every decision is taken and implemented by the individual central banks, which act by virtue of the political orientation present to the government and following the guidelines of the international central banks.

3.4.2 – The economy

Traders must also base their analysis on the dynamics that determine the economic performance of a nation or group of nations. This type of analysis must be based on all the social and political factors that characterize a territory, but also on the level of national consumption and the various productive sectors. Therefore, the economy is one of the pillars that support the entire Fundamental Analysis of Forex and, in order to analyze it in-depth, the trader will have to devote a lot of time to this phase of the analysis, or rely on data that are already ready, but which could turn out to be misinterpreted or incomplete.

3.4.3 – The trend in gold and oil commodities

Gold and oil are the commodities that most influence the financial sector and the Forex market. They are two elements often underestimated, neglected and not understood within the analysis, but in reality, they are crucial to understanding what the future trend of the trends may be.

In fact, gold is considered the refuge good par excellence. This means that traders, in the event that the markets go through some negative phases, try to invest in gold. For this reason, therefore, while all financial instruments show a negative trend, gold appears to be the only element to present a positive trend. Conversely, gold shows a downward trend when the market is experiencing moments of euphoria.

Oil is also one of the commodities that most influence the markets around the world and in particular the Forex. There are two different types of oil, but the advice is to focus attention on West Texas Intermediate, also known as WTI, which has a greater influence than Brent.

In fact, almost all world economies depend on oil, either because they import it or because they export it, and consequently this importance inevitably spills over into the financial market. A drop in oil prices, therefore, would entail advantages for importing countries and a disadvantage for exporting countries, and vice versa.

Conclusions

The topics discussed so far have allowed us to learn the main notions of Fundamental Analysis and what it entails. It is based on a series of simple principles, but difficult to apply if you do not have the necessary skills. To undertake the Fundamental Analysis, it is important to learn to examine the data of the financial statements of the companies to be able to make estimates and forecasts of short, medium and long term. The collection and the study of the great amount of financial data require quite long times and valid knowledge of the market and of the mathematical and econometric disciplines, which is why the Fundamental Analysis is not easy to use by the less experienced. But, if used correctly, it can guarantee optimal and optimized management of its capital, in such a way that it is invested by reducing risks and based on market volatility, with awareness and avoiding making wrong choices that would lead to the loss of money.

The cardinal principles of Fundamental Analysis are also useful for technical analysts as support tools in investment decisions, thanks to the study of the calendar of macroeconomic events to establish what is the most appropriate time to make investments.

Therefore, the Fundamental Analysis is a valid instrument, even if it presents some limits connected to its complexity, but it remains however very important to fully understand the financial markets.

www.ingramcontent.com/pod-product-compliance
Lightning Source LLC
Chambersburg PA
CBHW060849220526
45466CB00003B/1305

www.ingramcontent.com/pod-product-compliance
Lightning Source LLC
Chambersburg PA
CBHW060849220526
45466CB00003B/1305